IT
WORKS

SIMPLE SUCCESS GUIDES

How to Live on 24 Hours a Day
The Game of Life and How to Play It
The Go-Getter
The Golden Key
Dream Big
Simple Success and How to Attract Money

IT
WORKS

The Famous Little Red Book That Makes Your Dreams Come True

The Complete Original Edition

R. H. JARRETT

ST. MARTIN'S
ESSENTIALS
NEW YORK

Published in the United States by St. Martin's Essentials, an imprint of St. Martin's Publishing Group

INTRODUCTION. Copyright © 2023 by Joel Fotinos. All rights reserved. Printed in the United States of America. For information, address St. Martin's Publishing Group, 120 Broadway, New York, NY 10271.

www.stmartins.com

The Library of Congress Cataloging-in-Publication Data is available upon request.

ISBN 978-1-250-89778-7 (trade paperback)
ISBN 978-1-250-89779-4 (ebook)

Our books may be purchased in bulk for promotional, educational, or business use. Please contact your local bookseller or the Macmillan Corporate and Premium Sales Department at 1-800-221-7945, extension 5442, or by email at MacmillanSpecialMarkets@macmillan.com.

It Works was first published in 1926.
The Magic Story was first published in 1908.

First St. Martin's Essentials Trade Paperback Edition: 2023

10 9 8 7 6 5 4 3 2 1

This edition seeks to faithfully reproduce the original publications of the author's works and so has maintained the original spelling and grammar throughout, with only minor alterations for clarity or content.

CONTENTS

INTRODUCTION

It Works may be small in size, but it is giant in impact. Originally published in 1926, this little pamphlet has gone on to sell millions of copies and influence countless lives. *It Works* was written by Roy Herbert Jarrett (1874–1937), a sales executive based in Chicago who was interested in using metaphysical principles to gain abundance and prosperity in every area of life. His writing became not only popular, but iconic, in the area of mental success.

Rather than spend hundreds of pages on explanation and exposition, Jarrett boiled down his main principles to their most potent. One might easily be fooled by the small size of the content, but if you practice what he proposes, exactly as he proposes, then you will likely experience more success in whatever area you focus on.

I first encountered *It Works* back in the 1990s, when I worked for a popular bookstore in the

Midwest. Customer after customer would come in and ask for "the little red book." At first, I had no idea what they were talking about, but I quickly learned that they wanted a copy of the pamphlet *It Works* by R. H. Jarrett. I was intrigued, and finally decided to read it for myself. I was amazed by the depth beneath the simplicity of the message. It's clear that Jarrett's material was well-tested before he ever put it down on paper.

Part of the Simple Success Guides series, this St. Martin's Essentials edition contains the full and complete original edition of the pamphlet. This edition also includes additional features to supplement what you'll learn from R. H. Jarrett.

First is *The Magic Story* by Frederick Van Rensselaer Dey. This classic fable has been the inspiration for those looking for more growth and success in business and in life since it was originally published in 1900. Like *It Works*, *The Magic Story* is an early variation on the theme of the Law of Attraction. While not as famous as similar books like *It Works* and *Think and Grow Rich* by Napoleon Hill, *The Magic Story* has been influential over the decades and is experiencing a resurgence due to its message of positivity and inspiration.

We have also added a number of motivational poems and quotes. These materials are meant to augment the pamphlet's message, and have been foundational for millions of people looking for inspiration over the last century.

My hope is that you will read and enjoy *It Works* with an open mind, and then try out Jarrett's methods for yourself, remembering to follow whatever prompts Life presents to you. I might suggest that you read *It Works*, make your plan, and then begin to implement its main principles. As you do, allow *The Magic Story* and the poems to inspire you along the way. In this way, the two parts of the book—*It Works* and the supplemental materials—can work together to help you stay focused on receiving the most positive experiences possible.

As always, with these writings from the late nineteenth and early twentieth centuries, the language is of its time. While we want to acknowledge the limitations of the language here, we have not updated the material, choosing instead to leave the works in their original forms.

A final word of advice: make this book your own. We each are responsible for our own response to life, and this book teaches powerful techniques that can help to create a life of positivity and abundance if you use them in the spirit with which they were written. As the title suggests, *It Works* has worked for many before you, and now these same principles are waiting to help you to experience the life you desire.

—*Joel Fotinos*

IT
WORKS

To RHJ

"IT WORKS"

Before this book even had a title, the author sent the manuscript to a friend for an opinion to see what others thought. The friend returned it with a very simple notation, "It Works." Thus, this small booklet was born of experience and results.

RHJ was highly successful and widely known for his generosity and helpful spirit. He gave full credit for all that he accomplished in mastering circumstances, accumulating wealth and winning friends by quietly adopting the simple, powerful truth which he shared in his work. Here is an easy, open road to a larger, happier life. The author preferred that his name be omitted, knowing that the greatest good comes from helping others without expecting praise.

—Publisher

IT WORKS

A concise, definite, resultful plan with rules, explanations and suggestions for bettering your condition in life.

If you KNOW what you
WANT you can HAVE IT

WHAT IS THE REAL SECRET OF OBTAINING DESIRABLE POSSESSIONS?

ARE some people born under a lucky star or other charm which enables them to have all that which seems so desirable, and if not, what is the cause of the difference in conditions under which men live?

Many years ago, feeling that there must be a logical answer to this question, I decided to find out, if possible, what it was. I found the answer to my own satisfaction, and for years, have given the information to others who have used it successfully.

From a scientific, psychological or theological viewpoint, some of the following statements may be interpreted as incorrect, but nevertheless, the plan has brought the results desired to those who have followed the simple instructions, and it is my sincere belief that I am now presenting it in a way which will bring happiness and possessions to many more.

"IF wishes were horses, beggars would ride," is the attitude taken by the average man and woman in regard to possessions. They are not aware of *a power* so near that it is overlooked; so simple in operation that it is difficult to conceive; and so sure in results that it is not made use of consciously, or recognized as *the cause of failure or success.*

"GEE, I wish that were mine," is the outburst of Jimmy, the office boy, as a new red roadster goes by; and Florence, the telephone operator, expresses the same thought regarding a ring in the jeweler's window; while poor old Jones, the bookkeeper, during the Sunday stroll, replies to his wife, "Yes, dear, it would be nice to have a home like that, but it is out of the question. We will have to continue to rent." Landem, the salesman, protests that he does all the work, gets the short end of the money and will some day quit his job and find a real one, and President Bondum, in his private sanctorum, voices a bitter tirade against the annual attack of hay-fever.

At home it is much the same. Last evening, father declared that daughter Mabel was headed straight for disaster, and today, mother's allowance problem and other trying affairs fade into insignificance as she exclaims, "This is the last straw. Robert's school teacher wants to see me this afternoon. His reports are terrible, I know, but I'm late for Bridge now. She'll have to wait until tomorrow." So goes the endless stream of expressions like these from millions of people in all classes who give no thought to what they really want, *and who are getting all they are entitled to or expect.*

If you are one of these millions of thoughtless talkers or wishers and would like a decided change from your present condition, you can have it; but first of all you must *know what you want* and this is no easy task. When you can train your *objective mind* (the mind you use every day) to decide definitely upon the things or conditions you desire, you will have taken your first big step in accomplishing or securing what you know you want.

To get what you want is no more mysterious or uncertain than the radio waves all around you. Tune in correctly and you get a perfect result, but to do this, it is, of course, necessary to know something of your equipment and have a plan of operation.

You have within you a *mighty power*, anxious and willing to serve you, a *power capable* of giving you *that which you earnestly desire*. This power is described by Thomson Jay Hudson, Ph.D., LL.D., author of "The Law of Psychic Phenomena," as your *subjective mind*. Other learned writers use different names and terms, *but all agree that it is omnipotent*. Therefore, I call this Power "Emmanuel" (God in us).

Regardless of the name of this Great Power, or the conscious admission of a God, the Power is *capable and willing* to carry to a complete and perfect conclusion every earnest desire of your objective mind, but you must be really in earnest about what you want.

Occasional wishing or half-hearted wanting does not form a perfect connection or communication with *your omnipotent power*. You must be in earnest, *sincerely* and *truthfully* desiring certain conditions or things—mental, physical or spiritual.

Your objective mind and will are so vacillating that you usually only WISH for things and the wonderful, capable power within you does not function.

Most wishes are simply vocal expressions. Jimmy, the office boy, gave no thought of possessing the red roadster. Landem, the salesman, was not thinking of any other job or even thinking at all. President Bondum knew he had hay fever and was expecting it. Father's business was quite likely successful, and mother no doubt brought home first prize from the Bridge party that day, but they had no fixed idea of what they really wanted their children to accomplish and were actually helping to bring about the unhappy conditions which existed.

If you are in earnest about changing your present condition, here is a *concise, definite, resultful plan, with rules, explanations and suggestions.*

THE PLAN

WRITE down on paper in order of their importance the things and conditions you really want. Do not be afraid of wanting too much. Go the limit in writing down your wants. Change the list daily, adding to or taking from it, until you have it about right. Do not be discouraged on account of changes, as this is natural. There will always be changes and additions with accomplishments and increasing desires.

THREE POSITIVE RULES OF ACCOMPLISHMENT

1. *Read the list of what you want three times each day: morning, noon and night.*
2. *Think of what you want as often as possible.*
3. *Do not talk to any one about your plan except to the Great Power within you which will unfold to your Objective Mind the method of accomplishment.*

It is obvious that you cannot acquire faith at the start. Some of your desires, from all practical reasoning, may seem positively unattainable, but, nevertheless, write them down on your list in their proper place of importance to you.

There is no need to analyze how this Power within you is going to accomplish your desires. Such a procedure is as unnecessary as trying to figure out why a grain of corn placed in fertile soil shoots up a green stalk, blossoms and produces an ear of corn containing hundreds of grains, each capable of doing what the one grain did. If you will follow this definite plan and carry out the three simple rules, the method of accomplishment will unfold quite as mysteriously as the ear of corn appears on the stalk, and in most cases much sooner than you expect.

When new desires, deserving position at or about the top of your list, come to you, then you may rest assured you are progressing correctly.

Removing from your list items which at first you thought you wanted, *is another sure indication of progress.*

It is natural to be skeptical and have doubts, distrust and questionings, but when these thoughts arise, get out your list. Read it over; or if you have it memorized, talk to your inner self about your desires until the doubts that interfere with your progress are gone. *Remember, nothing can prevent your having that which you earnestly desire.* Others have these things. Why not you?

The Omnipotent Power within you does not enter into any controversial argument. *It is waiting and willing to serve when you are ready,* but your objective mind is so susceptible to suggestion that it is almost impossible to make any satisfactory progress when surrounded by skeptics. Therefore, choose your friends carefully and associate with people who now have some of the things you really want, but *do not discuss your method of accomplishment with them.*

Put down on your list of wants such material things as money, home, automobile, or whatever it may be, but do not stop there. Be more definite. If you want an automobile, decide *what kind, style, price, color,* and all the other details, including *when* you want it. If you want a home, plan the structure, grounds and furnishings. Decide on location and cost. If you want money, write down the amount. If you want to break a record in your business, put it down. It may be a sales record. If so, write out the total, the date required, then the number of items you must sell to make it, also list your prospects and put after each name the sum expected. This may seem very foolish at first, but you can never realize your desires if you do not *know positively and in detail what you want and when you want it.* If you cannot decide this, you are not in earnest. You must be definite, and when you are, results will be surprising and almost unbelievable.

A natural and ancient enemy will no doubt appear when you get your first taste of accomplishment. This enemy is Discredit, in form of such thoughts as: "It can't be possible; it just happened to be. What a remarkable coincidence!"

When such thoughts occur *give thanks and assert credit to your Omnipotent Power* for the accomplishment. By doing this, you gain assurance and more accomplishment, and in time, prove to yourself that *there is a law, which actually works—at all times*—when you are in tune with it.

Sincere and earnest thanks cannot be given without gratitude and it is impossible to be thankful and grateful without being happy. Therefore, when you are thanking your greatest and best friend, *your Omnipotent Power,* for the gifts received, do so *with all your soul, and let it be reflected in your face.* The Power and what it does is beyond understanding. Do not try to understand it, but *accept the accomplishment* with thankfulness, happiness, and strengthened faith.

Caution

It is possible to want and obtain that which will make you miserable; that which will wreck the happiness of others; that which will cause sickness and death; that which will rob you of eternal life. You can have what you want, but you must take all that goes with it: so in planning your wants, *plan that which you are sure will give to you and your fellow man the greatest good here on earth; thus paving the way to that future hope beyond the pale of human understanding.*

This method of securing what you want applies to everything you are capable of desiring and the scope being so great, it is suggested that your first list consist of only those things with which you are quite familiar, such as an amount of money or accomplishment, or the possession of material things. Such desires as these are more easily and quickly obtained than the discontinuance of fixed habits, the welfare of others, and the healing of mental or bodily ills.

Accomplish the lesser things first. Then take the next step, and when that is accomplished, you will seek the higher and really important objectives in life, but long before you reach this stage of your progress, many worthwhile desires will find their place on your list. One will be to help others as you have been helped. *Great is the reward to those who help and give without thought of self as it is impossible to be unselfish without gain.*

IN CONCLUSION

Ashort while ago, Dr. Emil Coué came to this country and showed thousands of people how to help themselves. Thousands of others spoofed at the idea, refused his assistance and are today where they were before his visit.

So with the statements and plan presented to you now. You can reject or accept. You can remain as you are or *have anything you want.* The choice is yours, but God grant that you may find in this short volume the inspiration to choose aright, follow the plan and thereby obtain, as so many others have, all things, whatever they may be, that you desire.

Read the entire book over again, *and again,* AND THEN AGAIN.

Memorize the three simple rules on pages thirteen and fourteen.

Test them now on what you want most *this minute.*

This book could have extended easily over 350 pages, but it has been deliberately shortened to make it as easy as possible for you to read, understand and use. Will you try it? Thousands of bettered lives will testify to the fact that *It Works*.

A LETTER TO YOU

FROM THE AUTHOR

Dear Reader:

The great possessions of life are all GIFTS mysteriously bestowed: sight, hearing, aspiration, love or life itself.

The same is true of ideas—the richest of them are given to us, as for instance, the powerful idea which this book has given you. What are you going to do with it? Are you surprised when I tell you the most profitable thing you can do is to give it away?

You can do this in an easy and practical way by having this book sent to those you know who NEED IT. In this way, you can help in the distribution of this worthwhile effort to make the lives of others better and happier.

You know people who are standing still or who are worried and discouraged. This is your chance to HELP THEM HELP THEMSELVES. If you withhold this book from them you will lose the conscious satisfaction that comes from doing good. If you see that they get this book, then you put yourself in line with the Law of Life which says, "You get by giving," and you may rightly expect prosperity and achievement.

At the very least you will have the inner sense of having done a good deed with no hope of being openly thanked and your reward will come secretly in added power and larger life.

—*The Author*

THE
MAGIC
STORY

PREFACE

THIS wonderful little story, written by Frederic Van Rensselaer Dey, first appeared in the December, 1900, and January, 1901, issues of SUCCESS MAGAZINE. It created an immediate sensation, and urgent requests were made for its reprint in book form. A small edition of a little silver-gray book was published to meet these requests, and this, the First Edition, has virtually disappeared from sight. The fact that the publishers of SUCCESS MAGAZINE are in almost daily receipt of requests for additional copies, is sufficient evidence of the value placed by the holders of the original edition upon the copies in their possession, and of their desire to bring it to the attention of their friends; and the demand has now become so insistent as to lead to the production of this, the Second Edition.

Mr. Dey has woven into this story, in a remarkably effective way, some of the fundamental principles of the "New Thought Movement" which is sweeping over this country, and it is safe to say that the application of these principles, as outlined in the "Magic Story," will accomplish almost, if not quite, all that is herein claimed for them towards the up-building and development of a manly, self-reliant, *success-compelling* spirit.

Part One

I WAS sitting alone in the *café*, and had just reached for the sugar preparatory to putting it into my coffee. Outside, the weather was hideous. Snow and sleet came swirling down, and the wind howled frightfully. Every time the outer door opened, a draft of unwelcome air penetrated the uttermost corners of the room. Still, I was comfortable. The snow and sleet and wind conveyed nothing to me except an abstract thanksgiving that I was where it could not affect me. While I dreamed and sipped my coffee, the door opened and closed, and admitted—Sturtevant.

Sturtevant was an undeniable failure, but, withal, an artist of more than ordinary talent. He had, however, fallen into the rut traveled by ne'er-do-wells, and was out at the elbows as well as insolvent.

As I raised my eyes to Sturtevant's, I was conscious of mild surprise at the change in his appearance. Yet he was not dressed differently. He wore the same threadbare coat in which he always appeared, and the old brown hat was the same. And yet there was something new and strange in his appearance. As he swished his hat around to relieve it of the burden of snow deposited by the howling nor'-wester, there was something new in the gesticulation. I could not remember when I had invited Sturtevant to dine with me, but involuntarily I beckoned to him. He nodded, and presently seated himself opposite to me. I asked him what he would have, and he, after scanning the bill of fare carelessly, ordered from it leisurely, and invited me to join him in coffee for two. I watched him in stupid wonder, but, as I had invited the obligation, I was prepared to pay for it, although I knew I hadn't sufficient cash to settle the bill. Meanwhile, I noted the brightness of his usual lackluster eyes, and the healthful, hopeful glow upon his cheek, with increasing amazement.

"Have you lost a rich uncle?" I asked.

"No," he replied, calmly, "but I have found my mascot."

"Brindle bull, or terrier?" I inquired.

"Currier," said Sturtevant, at length, pausing with his coffee cup half way to his lips, "I see that I have surprised you. It is not strange, for I am a surprise to myself. I am a new man, a different man,—and the alteration has taken place in the last few hours. You have seen me come into this place 'broke' many a time, when you have turned away, so that I would think you did not see me. I knew why you did that. It was not because you did not want to pay for a dinner, but because you did not have the money to do it. Is that your check? Let me have it. Thank you. I haven't any money with me tonight, but I,—well, this is my treat."

He called the waiter to him, and, with an in-imitable flourish, signed his name on the backs of the two checks, and waved him away. After that he was silent a moment while he looked into my eyes, smiling at the astonishment which I in vain strove to conceal.

"Do you know an artist who possesses more talent than I?" he asked, presently. "No. Do you happen to know anything in the line of my pro-fession that I could not accomplish, if I applied myself to it? No. You have been a reporter on the dailies for—how many?—seven or eight years.

Do you remember when I ever had any credit until to-night? No. Was I refused just now? You have seen for yourself. To-morrow my new career begins. Within a month I shall have a bank account. Why? Because I have discovered the secret of success."

"Yes," he continued, when I did not reply, "my fortune is made. I have been reading a strange story, and, since reading it, I feel that my fortune is assured. It will make your fortune, too. All you have to do is to read it. You have no idea what it will do for you. Nothing is impossible after you know that story. It makes everything as plain as A, B, C. The very instant you grasp its true meaning, success is certain. This morning I was a hopeless, aimless bit of garbage in the metropolitan ash can; to-night I wouldn't change places with a millionaire. That sounds foolish, but it is true. The millionaire has spent his enthusiasm; mine is all at hand."

"You amaze me," I said, wondering if he had been drinking absinthe. "Won't you tell me the story? I should like to hear it."

"Certainly. I mean to tell it to the whole world. It is really remarkable that it should have been written and should remain in print so long, with never a soul to appreciate it until now. This morning I was starving. I hadn't any credit, nor a place to get a meal. I was seriously meditating suicide. I had gone to three of the papers for which I had done work, and had been handed back all that I had submitted. I had to choose quickly between death by suicide and death slowly by starvation. Then I found the story and read it. You can hardly imagine the transformation. Why, my dear boy, everything changed at once,—and there you are."

"But what is the story, Sturtevant?"

"Wait; let me finish. I took those same old drawings to other editors, and every one of them was accepted at once."

"Can the story do for others what it has done for you? For example, would it be of assistance to me?" I asked.

"Help you? why not? Listen and I will tell it to you, although, really, you should read it. Still, I will tell it as best I can. It is like this: you see,————"

The waiter interrupted us at that moment. He informed Sturtevant that he was wanted at the telephone, and, with a word of apology, the artist left the table. Five minutes later I saw him rush out into the sleet and wind and disappear.

Within the recollection of the frequenters of that *café*, Sturtevant had never before been called out by telephone. That, of itself, was substantial proof of a change in his circumstances.

One night, on the street, I encountered Avery, a former college chum, then a reporter on one of the evening papers. It was about a month after my memorable interview with Sturtevant, which, by that time, was almost forgotten.

"Hello, old chap," he said; "how's the world using you? Still on space?"

"Yes," I replied, bitterly, "with prospects of being on the town, shortly. But you look as if things were coming your way. Tell me all about it."

"Things have been coming my way, for a fact, and it is all remarkable, when all is said. You know Sturtevant, don't you? It's all due to him. I was plumb down on my luck,—thinking of the morgue and all that,—looking for you, in fact, with the idea that you would lend me enough to pay my room rent, when I met Sturtevant. He told me a story, and, really, old man, it is the most remarkable story you ever heard; it made a new man of me. Within twenty-four hours I was on my feet, and I've hardly known a care or a trouble since."

Avery's statement, uttered calmly, and with the air of one who had merely pronounced an axiom, recalled to my mind the conversation with Sturtevant in the *café* that stormy night, nearly a month before.

"It must be a remarkable story," I said, incredulously. "Sturtevant mentioned it to me once. I have not seen him since. Where is he now?"

"He has been making war sketches in Cuba, at two hundred a week; he's just returned. It is a fact that everybody that has heard that story has done well since. There are Cosgrove and Phillips,—friends of mine,—you don't know them. One's a real estate agent; the other a broker's clerk. Sturtevant told them the story, and they have experienced the same results that I have; and they are not the only ones, either."

"Do you know the story?" I asked. "Will you try its effect on me?"

"Certainly; with the greatest pleasure in the world. I would like to have it printed in big black type, and posted on the elevated stations throughout New York. It certainly would do a lot of good, and it's as simple as A, B, C; like living on a farm. Excuse me a minute, will you? I see Danforth over there. Back in a minute, old chap."

He nodded and smiled,—and was gone. I saw him join the man whom he had designated as Danforth. My attention was distracted for a moment, and, when I looked again, both had disappeared.

If the truth be told, I was hungry. My pocket at that moment contained exactly five cents; just enough to pay my fare up-town, but insufficient also to stand the expense of filling my stomach. There was a "night owl" wagon in the neighborhood, where I had frequently "stood up" the purveyor of midnight dainties, and to him I applied. He was leaving the wagon as I was on the point of entering it, and I accosted him.

"I'm broke again," I said, with extreme cordiality. "You'll have to trust me once more. Some ham and eggs, I think, will do for the present."

He coughed, hesitated a moment, and then re-entered the wagon with me.

"Mr. Currier is good for anything he orders," he said to the man in charge; "one of my old customers. This is Mr. Bryan, Mr. Currier. He will take good care of you, and 'stand for' you, just the same as I would. The fact is, I have sold out. I've just turned over the outfit to Bryan. By the way, isn't Mr. Sturtevant a friend of yours?"

I nodded. I couldn't have spoken if I had tried.

"Well," continued the ex-"night owl" man, "he came here one night, about a month ago, and told me the most wonderful story I ever heard. I've just bought a place in Eighth Avenue, where I am going to run a regular restaurant—near Twenty-third Street. Come and see me."

He was out of the wagon, and the sliding door had been banged shut before I could stop him; so I ate my ham and eggs in silence, and resolved that I would hear that story before I slept. In fact, I began to regard it with superstition. If it had made so many fortunes, surely it should be capable of making mine.

The certainty that the wonderful story—I began to regard it as magic,—was in the air, possessed me. As I started to walk homeward, fingering the solitary nickel in my pocket and contemplating the certainty of riding down town in the morning, I experienced the sensation of something stealthily pursuing me, as if Fate were treading along behind me, yet never overtaking, and I was conscious that I was possessed with or by the story. When I reached Union Square, I examined my address book for the home of Sturtevant. It was not recorded there. Then I remembered the *café* in University place, and, although the hour was late, it occurred to me that he might be there.

He was! In a far corner of the room, surrounded by a group of acquaintances, I saw him. He discovered me at the same instant, and motioned to me to join them at the table. There was no chance for the story, however. There were half a dozen around the table, and I was the farthest removed from Sturtevant. But I kept my eyes upon him, and bided my time, determined that, when he rose to depart, I would go with him. A silence, suggestive of respectful awe, had fallen upon the party when I took my seat. Every one seemed to be thinking, and the attention of all was fixed upon Sturtevant. The cause was apparent. He had been telling the story. I had entered the *café* just too late to hear it. On my right, when I took my seat, was a doctor; on my left a lawyer. Facing me on the other side was a novelist with whom I had some acquaintance. The others were artists and newspaper men.

"It's too bad, Mr. Currier," remarked the doctor; "you should have come a little sooner.

Sturtevant has been telling us a story; it is quite wonderful, really. I say, Sturtevant, won't you tell that story again, for the benefit of Mr. Currier?"

"Why, yes. I believe that Currier has, somehow, failed to hear the magic story, although, as a matter of fact, I think he was the first one to whom I mentioned it at all. It was here, in this *café*, too,—at this very table. Do you remember what a wild night that was, Currier? Wasn't I called to the telephone, or something like that? To be sure! I remember, now; interrupted just at the point when I was beginning the story. After that, I told it to three or four fellows, and it 'braced them up,' as it had me. It seems incredible that a mere story can have such a tonic effect upon the success of so many persons who are engaged in such widely different occupations, but that is what it has done. It is a kind of neverfailing remedy, like a cough mixture that is warranted to cure everything, from a cold in the head to galloping consumption. There was Parsons, for example. He is a broker, you know, and had been on the wrong side of the market for a month. He had utterly lost his grip, and was on the verge of failure. I happened to meet him at the time he was feeling the bluest, and, before we parted, something brought me around to the subject of the story, and I related it to him. It had the same effect upon him that it had on me, and has had upon everybody who has heard it, as far as I know. I think you will all agree with me, that it is not the story itself that performs the surgical operation on the minds of those who are familiar with it; it is the way it is told,—in print, I mean. The author has, somehow, produced a psychological effect which is indescribable. The reader is hypnotized. He receives a mental and moral tonic. Perhaps, doctor, you can give some scientific explanation of the influence exerted by the story. It is a sort of elixir manufactured out of words, eh?"

From that the company entered upon a general discussion of theories. Now and then slight references were made to the story itself, and they were just sufficient to tantalize me,—the only one present who had not heard it.

At length, I left my chair, and, passing around the table, seized Sturtevant by one arm, and succeeded in drawing him away from the party.

"If you have any consideration for an old friend who is rapidly being driven mad by the existence of that confounded story, which Fate seems determined that I shall never hear, you will relate it to me now," I said, savagely.

Sturtevant stared at me in mild surprise.

"All right," he said. "The others will excuse me for a few moments, I think. Sit down here, and you shall have it. I found it pasted in an old scrapbook I purchased in Ann Street, for three cents; and there isn't a thing about it by which one can get any idea in what publication it originally appeared, or who wrote it. When I discovered it, I began casually to read it, and in a moment I was interested. Before I left it, I had read it through many times, so that I could repeat it almost word for word. It affected me strangely,—as if I had come in contact with some strong personality. There seems to be in the story a personal element that applies to every one who reads it. Well, after I had read it several times, I began to think it over. I couldn't stay in the house, so I seized my coat and hat and went out. I must have walked several miles, buoyantly, without realizing that I was the same man who, only a short time before, had been in the depths of despondency. That was the day I met you here,—you remember."

We were interrupted at that instant by a uniformed messenger, who handed Sturtevant a telegram. It was from his chief, and demanded his instant attendance at the office. The messenger had already been delayed an hour, and there was no help for it; he must go at once.

"Too bad!" said Sturtevant, rising and extending his hand. "Tell you what I'll do, old chap. I'm not likely to be gone any more than an hour or two. You take my key and wait for me in my room. In the *escritoire* near the window you will find an old scrapbook, bound in rawhide. It was manufactured, I have no doubt, by the author of the magic story. Wait for me in my room until I return."

With that he went out, and I lost no time in taking advantage of the permission he had given me.

I found the book without difficulty. It was a quaint, home-made affair, covered, as Sturtevant had said, with rawhide, and bound with leather thongs. The pages formed an odd combination of yellow paper, vellum and home-made parchment. I found the story, curiously printed on the last-named material. It was quaint and strange. Evidently, the printer had "set" it under the supervision of the writer. The phraseology was an unusual combination of seventeenth and eighteenth century mannerisms, and the interpolation of Italics and capitals could have originated in no other brain than that of its author.

In reproducing the following story, the peculiarities of type, spelling, etc., are eliminated, but in other respects it remains unchanged.

Part Two

Inasmuch as I have evolved from my experience the one great secret of success for all worldly undertakings, I deem it wise, now that the number of my days is nearly counted, to give to the generations that are to follow me the benefit of whatsoever knowledge I possess. I do not apologize for the manner of my expression, nor for lack of literary merit, the latter being, I wot, its own apology. Tools much heavier than the pen have been my portion, and, moreover, the weight of years has somewhat palsied hand and brain; nevertheless, the fact I can tell, and that I deem the meat within the nut. What mattereth it, in what manner the shell be broken, so that the meat be obtained and rendered useful? I doubt not that I shall use, in the telling, expressions that have clung to my memory since childhood; for, when men attain the number of my years, happenings of youth are like to be clearer to their perceptions than are events of recent date; nor doth it matter much how a thought is expressed, if it be wholesome and helpful, and findeth the understanding.

Much have I wearied my brain anent the question, how best to describe this recipe for success that I have discovered, and it seemeth advisable to give it as it came to me; that is, if I relate somewhat of the story of my life, the directions for agglomerating the substances, and supplying the seasoning for the accomplishment of the dish, will plainly be perceived. Happen they may; and that men may be born generations after I am dust, who will live to bless me for the words I write.

My father, then, was a seafaring man who, early in life, forsook his vocation, and settled on a plantation in the colony of Virginia, where, some years thereafter, I was born, which event took place in the year 1642; and that was over a hundred years ago. Better for my father had it been, had he hearkened to the wise advice of my mother, that he remain in the calling of his education; but he would not have it so, and the good vessel he captained was bartered for the land I spoke of. Here beginneth the first lesson to be acquired:—

Man should not be blinded to whatsoever merit exists in the opportunity which he bath in hand, remembering that a thousand promises for the future should weigh as naught against the possession of a single piece of silver.

When I had achieved ten years, my mother's soul took flight, and two years thereafter my worthy father followed her. I, being their only begotten, was left alone; howbeit, there were friends who, for a time, cared for me; that is to say, they offered me a home beneath their roof,—a thing which I took advantage of for the space of five months. From my father's estate there came to me naught; but, in the wisdom that came with increasing years, I convinced myself that his friend, under whose roof I lingered for some time, had defrauded him, and therefore me.

Of the time from the age of twelve and a half until I was three and twenty, I will make no recital here, since that time hath naught to do with this tale; but some time after, having in my possession the sum of sixteen guineas, ten, which I had saved from the fruits of my labor, I took ship to Boston town, where I began work first as a cooper, and thereafter as a ship's carpenter, although always after the craft was docked; for the sea was not amongst my desires.

Fortune will sometimes smile upon an intended victim because of pure perversity of temper. Such was one of my experiences. I prospered, and, at seven and twenty, owned the yard wherein, less than four years earlier, I had worked for hire. Fortune, howbeit, is a jade who must be coerced; she will not be coddled. Here beginneth the second lesson to be acquired:

Fortune is ever elusive, and can only be retained by force. Deal with her tenderly and she will forsake you for a stronger man. [In that, methinks, she is not unlike other women of my knowledge.]

About this time, Disaster (which is one of the heralds of broken spirits and lost resolve), paid me a visit. Fire ravaged my yards, leaving nothing in its blackened paths but debts, which I had not the coin wherewith to defray. I labored with my acquaintances, seeking assistance for a new start, but the fire that had burned my competence, seemed also to have consumed their sympathies. So it happened, within a short time, that not only had I lost all, but I was hopelessly indebted to others; and for that they cast me into prison. It is possible that I might have rallied from my losses but for this last indignity, which broke down my spirits so that I became utterly despondent. Upward of a year was I detained within the gaol; and, when I did come forth, it was not the same hopeful, happy man, content with his lot, and with confidence in the world and its people, who had entered there.

Life has many pathways, and of them by far the greater number lead downward. Some are precipitous, others are less abrupt; but ultimately, no matter at what inclination the angle may be fixed, they arrive at the same destination,—failure. And here beginneth the third lesson:

Failure exists only in the grave. Man, being alive, hath not yet failed; always he may turn about and ascend by the same path he descended by; and there may be one that is

less abrupt (albeit longer of achievement), and
more adaptable to his condition.

When I came forth from prison, I was penniless. In all the world I possessed naught beyond the poor garments which covered me, and a walking stick which the turnkey had permitted me to retain, since it was worthless. Being a skilled workman, howbeit, I speedily found employment at good wages; but, having eaten of the fruit of worldly advantage, dissatisfaction possessed me. I became morose and sullen; whereat, to cheer my spirits, and for the sake of forgetting the losses I had sustained, I passed my evenings at the tavern. Not that I drank overmuch of liquor, except on occasion (for I have ever been somewhat abstemious), but that I could laugh, and sing, and parry wit and *badinage* with my ne'er-do-well companions; and here might be included the fourth lesson:

Seek comrades among the industrious, for those
who are idle will sap your energies from you.

It was my pleasure at that time to relate, upon slight provocation, the tale of my disasters, and to rail against the men whom I deemed to have wronged me, because they had seen fit not to come to my aid. Moreover, I found childish delight in filching from my employer, each day, a few moments of the time for which he paid me. Such a thing is less honest than downright theft.

This habit continued and grew upon me until the day dawned which found me not only without employment, but also without character, which meant that I could not hope to find work with any other employer in Boston town.

It was then that I regarded myself a failure. I can liken my condition at that time for naught more similar than that of a man who, descending the steep side of a mountain, loses his foothold. The farther he slides, the faster he goes. I have also heard this condition described by the word Ishmaelite, which I understand to be a man whose hand is against everybody, and who thinks that the hands of every other man are against him; and here beginneth the fifth lesson:

The Ishmaelite and the leper are the same, since both are abominations in the sight of man,—albeit they differ much, in that the former may be restored to perfect health. The

former is entirely the result of imagination; the
latter has poison in his blood.

I will not discourse at length upon the gradual degeneration of my energies. It is not meet ever to dwell much upon misfortunes (which saying is also worthy of remembrance). It is enough if I add that the day came when I possessed naught wherewith to purchase food and raiment, and I found myself like unto a pauper, save at infrequent times when I could earn a few pence, or, mayhap, a shilling. Steady employment I could not secure, so I became emaciated in body, and naught but a skeleton in spirit.

My condition, then, was deplorable; not so much for the body, be it said, as for the mental part of me, which was sick unto death. In my imagination I deemed myself ostracised by the whole world, for I had sunk very low indeed; and here beginneth the sixth and final lesson to be acquired, (which cannot be told in one sentence, nor in one paragraph, but must needs be adapted from the remainder of this tale).

Well do I remember my awakening, for it came in the night, when, in truth, I did awake from sleep. My bed was a pile of shavings in the rear of the cooper shop where once I had worked for hire; my roof was the pyramid of casks, underneath which I had established myself. The night was cold, and I was chilled, albeit, paradoxically, I had been dreaming of light and warmth and of the repletion of good things. You will say, when I relate the effect the vision had on me, that my mind was affected. So be it, for it is the hope that the minds of others might be likewise influenced which disposes me to undertake the labor of this writing. It was the dream which converted me to the belief—nay, to the knowledge,—that I was possessed of two identities; and it was my own better self that afforded me the assistance for which I had pleaded in vain from my acquaintances. I have heard this condition described by the word "double." Nevertheless, that word does not comprehend my meaning. A double can be naught more than a double, neither half being possessed of individuality. But I will not philosophize, since philosophy is naught but a suit of garments for the decoration of a dummy figure.

Moreover, it was not the dream itself which

affected me; it was the impression made by it, and the influence that it exerted over me, which accomplished my enfranchisement. In a word, then, I encouraged my other identity. After toiling through a tempest of snow and wind, I peered into a window and saw that other being. He was rosy with health; before him, on the hearth, blazed a fire of logs; there was conscious power and force in his demeanor; he was physically and mentally muscular. I rapped timidly upon the door, and he bade me enter. There was a not unkindly smile of derision in his eyes as he motioned me to a chair by the fire; but he uttered no word of welcome; and, when I had warmed myself, I went forth again into the tempest, burdened with the shame which the contrast between us had forced upon me. It was then that I awoke; and here cometh the strange part of my tale, for, when I did awake, I was not alone. There was a Presence with me; intangible to others, I discovered later, but real to me.

The Presence was in my likeness, yet was it strikingly unlike. The brow, not more lofty than my own, yet seemed more round and full; the eyes, clear, direct, and filled with purpose, glowed with enthusiasm and resolution; the lips, chin,—ay, the whole contour of face and figure was dominant and determined.

He was calm, steadfast, and self-reliant; I was cowering, filled with nervous trembling, and fearsome of intangible shadows. When the Presence turned away, I followed, and throughout the day I never lost sight of it, save when it disappeared for a time beyond some doorway where I dared not enter; at such places, I awaited its return with trepidation and awe, for I could not help wondering at the temerity of the Presence (so like myself, and yet so unlike), in daring to enter where my own feet feared to tread.

It seemed also as if purposely, I was led to the place and to the men where, and before whom I most dreaded to appear; to offices where once I had transacted business; to men with whom I had financial dealings. Throughout the day I pursued the Presence, and at evening saw it disappear beyond the portals of a hostelry famous for its cheer and good living. I sought the pyramid of casks and shavings.

Not again in my dreams that night did I encounter the Better Self (for that is what I have named it), albeit, when, perchance, I awakened from slumber, it was near to me, ever wearing that calm smile of kindly derision which could not be mistaken for pity, nor for condolence in any form. The contempt of it stung me sorely.

The second day was not unlike the first, being a repetition of its forerunner, and I was again doomed to wait outside during the visits which the Presence paid to places where I fain would have gone had I possessed the requisite courage. It is fear which deporteth a man's soul from his body and rendereth it a thing to be despised. Many a time I essayed to address it but enunciation rattled in my throat, unintelligible; and the day closed like its predecessor.

This happened many days, one following another, until I ceased to count them; albeit, I discovered that constant association with the Presence was producing an effect upon me; and one night, when I awoke among the casks and discerned that he was present, I made bold to speak, albeit with marked timidity.

"Who are you?" I ventured to ask; and I was startled into an upright posture by the sound of my own voice; and the question seemed to give pleasure to my companion, so that I fancied there was less of derision in his smile when he responded.

"I am that I am," was the reply. "I am he who you have been; I am he who you may be again; wherefore do you hesitate? I am he who you were, and whom you have cast out for other company. I am the man made in the image of God, who once possessed your body. Once we dwelt within it together, not in harmony, for that can never be, nor yet in unity, for that is impossible, but as tenants in common who rarely fought for full possession. Then, you were a puny thing, but you became selfish and exacting until I could no longer abide with you, wherefore I stepped out. There is a plus-entity and a minus-entity in every human body that is born into the world. Whichever one of these is favored by the flesh becomes dominant; then is the other inclined to abandon its habitation, temporarily or for all time. I am the plus-entity of yourself; you are the minus-entity. I own all things; you possess naught. That body which we both inhabited is mine, but it is unclean, and I will not dwell within it. Cleanse it, and I will take possession."

"Why do you pursue me?" I next asked of the Presence.

"You have pursued me, not I you. You can exist without me for a time, but your path leads downward, and the end is death. Now that you approach the end, you debate if it be not politic that you should cleanse your house and invite me to enter. Step aside, then, from the brain and the will; cleanse them of your presence; only on that condition will I ever occupy them again."

"The brain hath lost its power," I faltered. "The will is a weak thing, now; can you repair them?"

"Listen!" said the Presence, and he towered over me while I cowered abjectly at his feet. "To the plus-entity of a man, all things are possible. The world belongs to him,—is his estate. He fears naught, dreads naught, stops at naught; he asks no privileges, but demands them; he *dominates*, and cannot cringe; his requests are orders; opposition flees at his approach; he levels mountains, fills in vales, and travels on an even plane where stumbling is unknown."

Thereafter, I slept again, and, when I awoke, I seemed to be in a different world. The sun was shining and I was conscious that birds twittered above my head. My body, yesterday trembling and uncertain, had become vigorous and filled with energy. I gazed upon the pyramid of casks in amazement that I had so long made use of it for an abiding place, and I was wonderingly conscious that I had passed my last night beneath its shelter.

The events of the night recurred to me, and I looked about me for the Presence. It was not visible, but anon I discovered, cowering in a far corner of my resting place, a puny, abject, shuddering figure, distorted of visage, deformed of shape, disheveled and unkempt of appearance. It tottered as it walked, for it approached me piteously; but I laughed aloud, mercilessly. Perchance I knew then that it was the minus-entity, and that the plus-entity was within me; albeit I did not then realize it. Moreover, I was in haste to get away; I had no time for philosophy. There was much for me to do,—much; strange it was that I had not thought of that yesterday. But yesterday was gone,—today was with me,—it had just begun.

As had once been my daily habit, I turned my steps in the direction of the tavern, where formerly I had partaken of my meals. I nodded cheerily as I entered, and smiled in recognition of returned salutations. Men who had ignored me for months bowed graciously when I passed them on the thoroughfare. I went to the washroom, and from there to the breakfast table; afterwards when I passed the taproom, I paused a moment and said to the landlord:

"I will occupy the same room that I formerly used, if, perchance, you have it at disposal. If not, another will do as well, until I can obtain it."

Then I went out and hurried with all haste to the cooperage. There was a huge wain in the yard, and men were loading it with casks for shipment. I asked no questions, but, seizing barrels, began hurling them to the men who worked atop of the load. When this was finished, I entered the shop. There was a vacant bench; I recognized its disuse by the litter on its top. It was the same at which I had once worked. Stripping off my coat, I soon cleared it of *impedimenta*. In a moment more I was seated, with my foot on the vice-lever, shaving staves.

It was an hour later when the master workman entered the room, and he paused in surprise at sight of me; already there was a goodly pile of neatly shaven staves beside me, for in those days I was an excellent workman; there was none better, but, alas! now, age hath deprived me of my skill. I replied to his unasked question with the brief, but comprehensive sentence: "I have returned to work, sir." He nodded his head and passed on, viewing the work of other men, albeit anon he glanced askance in my direction.

Here endeth the sixth and last lesson to be acquired, although there is more to be said, since from that moment I was a successful man, and ere long possessed another shipyard, and had acquired a full competence of worldly goods.

I pray you who read, heed well the following admonitions, since upon them depend the word "success" and all that it implies:

Whatsoever you desire of good is yours. You have but to stretch forth your hand and take it.

Learn that the consciousness of dominant power within you is the possession of all things attainable.

Have no fear of any sort or shape, for fear is an adjunct of the minus-entity.

If you have skill, apply it; the world must profit by it, and, therefore, you.

Make a daily and nightly companion of your plus-entity; if you heed its advice, you cannot go wrong.

Remember, philosophy is an argument; the world, which is your property, is an accumulation of facts.

Go, therefore, and do that which is within you to do; take no heed of gestures which would beckon you aside; *ask of no man permission to perform.*

The minus-entity requests favors; the plus-entity grants them. Fortune waits upon every footstep you take; seize her, bind her, hold her, for she is yours; she belongs to you.

Start out now, with these admonitions in your mind. Stretch out your hand, and grasp the plus, which, maybe, you have never made use of, save in grave emergencies. Life is an emergency most grave.

Your plus-entity is beside you now; cleanse your brain, and strengthen your will. It will take possession. It waits upon you.

Start to-night; start now upon this new journey.

Be always on your guard. Whichever entity controls you, the other hovers at your side; beware lest the evil enter, even for a moment.

My task is done. I have written the recipe for "success." If followed, it cannot fail. Wherein I may not be entirely comprehended, the plus-entity of whosoever reads will supply the deficiency; and upon that Better Self of mine, I place the burden of imparting to generations that are to come, the secret of this all-pervading good,—*the secret of being what you have it within you to be.*

ADDITIONAL
MATERIALS

"Opportunity" by Walter Malone

They do me wrong who say I come no more
When once I knock and fail to find you in;
For every day I stand outside your door,
And bid you wake, and rise to fight and win.

Wail not for precious chances passed away,
Weep not for golden ages on the wane!
Each night I burn the records of the day-
At sunrise every soul is born again!

Laugh like a boy at splendors that have sped,
To vanished joys be blind and deaf and dumb;
My judgements seal the dead past with its dead,
But never bind a moment yet to come.

Though deep in mire, wring not your hands and
    weep;
I lend my arm to all who say "I Can!"
No shame-faced outcast ever sank so deep,
But yet might rise and be again a man.

Dost thou behold thy lost youth all aghast?
Dost reel from righteous Retribution's blow?

Then turn from blotted archives of the past,
And find the future's pages white as snow.

Art thou a mourner? Rouse thee from thy spell;
Art thou a sinner? Sins may be forgiven;
Each morning gives thee wings to flee from hell,
Each night a star to guide thy feet to heaven.

"Preparedness" by Edwin Markham

For all your days prepare,
  And meet them ever alike:
When you are the anvil, bear —
  When you are the hammer, strike.

"Resolve" by Charlotte Perkins Gilman

To keep my health!
To do my work!
To live!
To see to it I grow and gain and give!
Never to look behind me for an hour!
To wait in weakness and to walk in power.
But always fronting onward toward the light
Always and always facing toward the right,
Robbed, starved, defeated, fallen, wide astray—
On with what strength I have
Back to the way!

"Wishing" by Ella Wheeler Wilcox

Do you wish the world were better?
Let me tell you what to do:
Set a watch for your actions,
Keep them always straight and true;
Rid your mind of selfish motives;
Let your thoughts be clean and high.
You can make a little Eden
Of the sphere you occupy.

Do you wish the world were wiser?
Well, suppose you made a start,
By accumulating wisdom
In the scrapbook of your heart:
Do not waste one page on folly;
Live to learn, and learn to live.
If you want to give men knowledge
You must get it, ere you give.

Do you wish the world were happy?
Then remember day by day
Just to scatter seeds of kindness
As you pass along the way;

For the pleasures of the many
May ofttimes traced to one,
As the hand that plants an acorn
Shelters armies from the sun.

"Success" by Berton Braley

If you want a thing bad enough
To go out and fight for it,
Work day and night for it,
Give up your time and your peace and your sleep
     for it
If only desire of it
Makes you quite mad enough
Never to tire of it,
Makes you hold all other things tawdry and
     cheap for it
If life seems all empty and useless without it
And all that you scheme and you dream is about it,
If gladly you'll sweat for it,
Fret for it,
Plan for it,
Lose all your terror of God or man for it,
If you'll simply go after that thing that you want,
With all your capacity,
Strength and sagacity,
Faith, hope and confidence, stern pertinacity,
If neither cold poverty, famished and gaunt,
Nor sickness nor pain

Of body or brain
Can turn you away from the thing that you want,
If dogged and grim you besiege and beset it,
You'll get it!

"My Wage" by Jessie B. Rittenhouse

I bargained with Life for a penny,
And Life would pay no more,
However I begged at evening
When I counted my scanty store;

For Life is a just employer,
He gives you what you ask,
But once you have set the wages,
Why, you must bear the task.

I worked for a menial's hire,
Only to learn, dismayed,
That any wage I had asked of Life,
Life would have paid.

"Success," from "The Ladder of St. Augustine" by Henry Wadsworth Longfellow

We have not wings, we cannot soar;
But we have feet to scale and climb
By slow degrees, by more and more,
The cloudy summits of our time.

The mighty pyramids of stone
That wedge-like cleave the desert airs,
When nearer seen and better known,
Are but gigantic flights of stairs.

The distant mountains, that uprear
Their solid bastions of the skies,
Are crossed by pathways that appear
As we to higher levels rise.

The heights by great men reached and kept
Were not attained by sudden flight,
But they, while their companions slept,
Were toiling upward in the night.

"I have not failed. I've just found 10,000 ways that won't work."

—Thomas Edison

"Twenty years from now you will be more disappointed by the things that you didn't do than by the ones you did do. So throw off the bowlines. Sail away from the safe harbor. Catch the trade winds in your sails. Explore. Dream. Discover."

—Mark Twain

"If—" by Rudyard Kipling

If you can keep your head when all about you
    Are losing theirs and blaming it on you,
If you can trust yourself when all men doubt you,
    But make allowance for their doubting too;
If you can wait and not be tired by waiting,
    Or being lied about, don't deal in lies,
Or being hated, don't give way to hating,
    And yet don't look too good, nor talk too wise:

If you can dream—and not make dreams your
    master;
    If you can think—and not make thoughts your
    aim;
If you can meet with Triumph and Disaster
    And treat those two impostors just the same;
If you can bear to hear the truth you've spoken
    Twisted by knaves to make a trap for fools,
Or watch the things you gave your life to, broken,
    And stoop and build 'em up with worn-out
    tools:

If you can make one heap of all your winnings
    And risk it on one turn of pitch-and-toss,

And lose, and start again at your beginnings
    And never breathe a word about your loss;
If you can force your heart and nerve and sinew
    To serve your turn long after they are gone,
And so hold on when there is nothing in you
    Except the Will which says to them: 'Hold on!'

If you can talk with crowds and keep your virtue,
    Or walk with Kings—nor lose the common
    touch,
If neither foes nor loving friends can hurt you,
    If all men count with you, but none too much;
If you can fill the unforgiving minute
    With sixty seconds' worth of distance run,
Yours is the Earth and everything that's in it,
    And—which is more—you'll be a Man, my son!